LONE YELLOW FLOWER

poems

LONE YELLOW FLOWER

Erika Gill

QUERENCIA

Querencia Press – Chicago IL

QUERENCIA PRESS

© Copyright 2025
Erika Gill
Cover Design: Danielle Camorlinga

Library of Congress Control Number: 2025934375

ISBN 978 1 963943 39 9

www.querenciapress.com

First Published in 2025

Querencia Press, LLC
Chicago IL

Printed & Bound in the United States of America

Erika Gill's *Lone Yellow Flower* is an act of rebellion and reclamation. The poet invites the reader to examine the personal and the political, orange juice and carcasses, blackberries and pandemics. Gill breathes poetry into the experiences of heartbreak and a world on fire. Their poetry comes defiantly out of the ashes of old dead white poets and living bloodthirsty oligarchs, certainly outlasting both. Above all, the poems in *Lone Yellow Flower* are beautiful songs of solidarity, resisting heart-eaters and refusing indifference for fellow humans. When grief feels insurmountable, these poems are a must-read.

— SG Huerta, author of *GOOD GRIEF* & *Burns*

Erika Gill's poetry vibe checks the pulse of us, writing of memorial spaces, aloneness and quiet with the affect of a warm window looking into a broken world. The inner monologue of this collection seems largely to have taken shape within the pandemic's gilded nature; Gill addresses death to come "by covid or cop / enlarged, encapsulating." They write of the heart, that they "never loved with that spare part." They write of ruined blackberries and carpets grieved deeply through the lens of reductive loss. Erika writes through a system of grieving with an open heart, reaching out, into and through the music of Phoebe Bridgers, through the blossoms growing in a neighbor's yard, and in contemplation of a greater good for justice. As the collection tapers away, we feel a sense of having been tapered ourselves; whittled down to our barest bone.

—Eszter Takacs, author of *Together We Will Talk Right Down to Earth* & *The Spectacular Crash*

CONTENTS

Epitome

The biggest joke deity ever played on me
was putting my soul into my model body.

Nearly five foot ten inches of light skin
green eyes straight teeth curly hair.
But what else is there?

I am library book pages browned with age
I am a cat's tail curled into a question mark
I am soul music and jazz beats
I am fireworks on The Fourth
leaving ghostly imprints in your eyes.

I am black power and white guilt,
I am promise and opportunity and crushing failure,
magazine pages, designer scent samples
and your moldy lunch leftovers in Tupperware.

I am the dynamite
and the leveled mountaintop.

I am America whether she wants me or not.

I am femininity in boudoir
and butch, masc, defiant in the street.

What I'm not is zeitgeist.
I'm not the "New" America.
My wounds are not new social ills
they're old furrows that have festered.
It's been a hundred fifty some-odd years of fallow fields
but my hands hold ghosts that plowed them
and ghosts that owned them,

and my hands cannot be put to rest.

What it is

I can't fathom showing you my sadness
an open wound that pulses
in time with the inner beat
yellow fatty layer exposed

What do our insides look like oxidized?
Has anyone been left open that long alive?

How can you who has never known
never been grasped and whispered at
shaken, pricked, spittled, immolated by shame
dug out of your den and flung far

scraped so that the flesh beneath
rich color, shows an alarm

never grayed in shock, vertigo
near-death
never frozen still with yawing emptiness
in the wake of a slap felt in your throat,

know with your bones, with the glide
of cartilage moved into determination

dry voiced, what it is
what it is

that incantation to repel
wickedest taboo
rules written in lemon juice
rubbed solicitously into flayed backs

an expectation of neat coils
cleaned, hung ready, on display
once owned, all inherit
but will never be acknowledged

and so my sadness is unknown to you
who pick carcasses clean
and all who endeavor to exist
outside the permeable lining of my mind.

Stargazing At The Lake

The lake at night is glossy and flat black
an obsidian mirror reflecting watercolor fingers
spears of light of the storefronts and homes and streetlights
the water beneath impenetrable and hard
empty without light

my heart craves the sight of this expanse
winter trees stretch skeleton fingers up, upward
yearning, as I begin, fearfully, to contemplate yearning
tightly closed petals slowly unfurl
mortally afraid of the frost, your indifference
but I sink slowly and warm into the depths of light-shot amber
chips
your eyes absorb it all and I sink in with a sigh
oh oh oh—
I sigh
warmth, light, a new star to orbit
I do my cosmic mating dance in an ellipse
uncertain if I should be near or far
wobbling unsteady, ever closer to your surface

I heard between your words the fear of being a satellite

I can't alter your gravity
but I can pull the shorelines into a script
that begs *love me, love me, love me*
and grip hard to draw the deep waters and gather them to me
like skirts
blanketed, robed in darkness to cover my violent glow
crowned in a fading light I hope you see
or put out, but soon.

Baggage

You're so loud
the timbre of you shouting resonates in my chest
I always chastise you, though I know the warmed up
smooth mechanics of vocal cords and metal heat expression
of letting it out, unstoppable—
"What do I owe you?!"
like my affection is a transaction

I don't want to be your friend
because my eye is drawn to your mouth
my heart skips to the marimba of your gait
because I want your eyes to close at the caress
each time I run my fingers through your hair

"Let's just call it, then."
like this tangled knot is a game
some sportsball fan whose team has lost
though, I did feel crushed much the same way
the league wouldn't worm its way deep
from my throat to my gut

you hold me so tight when I want you to let me go

you sing so sweet in my mind when I want you quiet
and so absent when I needed you to fill the hollow in my chest

I've grown weary of carrying the baggage you brought
from someone else
and someone else
—a short lifetime of someone elses
that act think sing dance love hate and burn
nothing like me

I'm the cherry hot coin you swallow
that will sear all its way down
when not cooled, immediately tempered by rejection

you can't know how it makes me feel
how I was waterlogged and charred
you cut me in half but didn't stay to count the rings
Was I a thing? Was I real?

Eat Here

If my anger were a meal
it would be warm venison and mashed potatoes
lukewarm,
gamy and hard to chew.

leaden in your stomach,
underseasoned, disappointing.

Plated sloppily on out of fashion flatware
which you've never seen before
because I only pull it out on special occasions
—but not when company is there.

It would only to be eaten slow,
utensils blocky and uncomfortable,
pressing against your bones
until your hands are sore from sawing
trying to get through to the bottom.

Endless sawing,
until you'd rather just push the plate away.
Leave it there for someone else to handle
and decide to take your hunger elsewhere.

Mouse Tea

My mother didn't know how to love me
with enough affection
hugs too strong-armed
infrequent

so I fortified myself maternally
with dime store paperbacks
by women who wrote boldly
and pedantic

the women who wrote characters
not insecurities
magic but no nonsense

who taught me things
crime scene etiquette
(always wear the booties)
that you can make a tea so strong
a mouse might walk on it

that swords can be heavy
how to curse and mean it

that there are men who will chase after
smart and witty and brazen

that you can love so hard it'll make you hurt
that you can break things
be broken
and keep a straight face through any insult
or wield your anger (and your tongue)
like a weapon.

Portrait of Anxiety (The Worm)

Reclined, indisposed
disinclined toward the chest's rise and fall
a pale worm in the sunlight
unwashed chicken skin,
filmed with incense smoke
shriveling into its clothes
a reflecting eye stares out
into the cast of late afternoon
drafty room and empty
the absent phalanges scratch
punitive scalp
spooling misery
dressed in dark clothing
with a liberal cat hair sprinkle
sigh shift and blink
the flesh, began to hang off the bones, as if aversion
and shame stretch the squamous
dissociation
the dermatillomania of thought
empty out the bottle,
a wealth of sanity in pink pill capsules
[custodial hands removed the caps of wounds]
Did it swallow down that pill today?
Did it drink enough water?

Bathe?
Remember to breathe.

Lie in state, the blind worm eating
fear flowers and choking them back up
graceful in repose
long limbs at a tipping point
on the run to fat
skin still glistening with waning shimmer
features still a fine construction
though, in holographic side view, hateful
   —curate it, quick!
   Carefully arranged, it will keep!
Fester, fester if left, if alone
too long without touch and sound
all fade, all fester—future tense
but now — O — what tableau
what surface gleam,
what beauty, what truth.
What fading strength.
Though, underneath,
on the psychic layer,
a hint—a waft
the smell of rot.

Pigeon's wing, torn off

—For Brandon Bernard

They killed a man today
today today today
and yesterday
gunshot or veinshot
a sandwich as a weapon
(outside of the vacuum of patriarchy)
we are inside
nine months now
and we have gestated nothing but rage
curdling impotent and impolite

I took a walk this afternoon and saw
a pigeon's wing torn off
grey like the day, glorious
as an angel's appendage
psychopomp disabled
and I limped along—temporary
too soon on my fixed knee?
I see things differently
the bare red branches of a bush
and seed pods dried and waiting
What will they be come spring?
I do not know and won't be there to see.

Howls Unheard

I can hardly bear to be in this city of Babylon.
I am not the first to compare
your towering walls to sprawling towns.
Greed, greed in the west.
I choke on modern decay
see the oil in the gutters coalesce,
the plaque in your arteries harden.
Slake your lust with eyes on pubescent flesh,
eat your children, swallow your fillings.
Or sell them both off to indecorous wars
fought with no handshakes.
Digest the news, consumed in micro-portions
wrapped up in one lettuce leaf.
Wash it down with diet and die
a slow death surrounded by friends,
all inanimate with indifferent faces.

Fester appendix

When I get my dirty hands on you
when I get my dirty hands

it grows in me
grows
to consume the body

my woman's heart, man's womb
all fester, all kneel

to consume the body.

Song in the key of Why?

There is a darkness within me,
a darkness
with my insides
a split open Swiss Roll,
the corn syrup solids spill out
a gelatinous fluff of lies and sins
I don't even believe in.

Years and years have passed but I still think of you,
though I hear no wedding bells in your name,
I'll send you a text on the anniversary of your
dear mother's death.

If only you could know,
if only you'd dare
respond, so I could tell you
I have become so much more
than I ever feared,
ever hated.

There was a darkness within me
and now it spills out

and I, a gutted fish,
still flapping, grow
grotesque, and the smell,
oh, the smell of it.

You'd be able to pick up on it in a second,
even with allergy muted senses, you always knew,
I think, knew deep down that there was something
muddy and twisted within me
and those tangles untangle in the bloating heat.

I've become many things, so many of them good,
wondrous fair, but you could still guess,
if you wanted, if you'd try,
you'd still see the darkness there.

J'ai peur de cet animal

I cannot revisit,

except in dreams,

these thoughts,

not visceral, even long past,

knife wounds,

a hunted feeling.

Velvet stalker in the shadow wears my face,

but my heart's a mallet,

my rib cage is meat tenderized

by the thought of delving in my own brain,

spelunking into those thoughts

gripping gossamer dendrite rope.

The fall will kill me.

I cannot revisit

the pain filled pages

with the impulse to marinate my nerves

with a clear liquor numb pour

deaden my circuitry, if it can't be cut off

I fear the thing itself,

The Dark Stranger,

the unknowable

deepness in me

that could chase away stronger minds in terror.

It is the animal that fears

the human in me.

I Sought Refuge Where The Rocks Cleft

I.

I awoke in the sunlight. My lips and cuticles,
the joinings of my skin, all cracked and ran.
Desperation in my folds, I sought refuge where the rocks
cleft.

I had been there before. The curious valley let me settle
into the sand,
raising little dust, but to cover me, make the scenery all
the same.
Coated by the granules embedded in my pores,
I grew bored and dreamt of escape.
I moved sluggishly, exhuming my sand-armored limbs
—made leathery by the salt earth.
I excavated myself
I began to climb.

The sides caved in as I was scrabbling
up, as sand will sometimes do.
You stood and watched my struggle, wondering
that I did not simply pick The Way That Leads Out.
I sat at the bottom for a while,

dumbfounded, until the sun rose high overhead.
I began to bake. The buzzards began to circle.

II.

It has been years now, and I have learned
this place is a mosaic; this valley
with its sky stretched heartbreakingly overhead,
with its clean drinking water,
spacious homes, ample parking.
One hundred thousand cars times
one hundred thousand spawn or spouses,
yield: one million some-odd reasons
why the skies are only clear some-times now,
and so many lives lured by its promise,
so many bones interred in its stillness.

I laid my heart bare and cooked the dense flesh of it
over the asphalt, watching the deep reds of it grow dusk
and beige.
He ate it, with knife and fork, staring into my eyes as he
chewed each bite,
pausing to wipe the juice running down his chin.

No matter, I have found it was a useless piece of me, now I
am dead.
Truth be told, I never loved with that spare part.

III.

If I am nobody, then you are too! Our white bones picked
clean
look all the same anyway, and we can hide our skulls and
their difference.
Mine, not collapsed at the fore, not cloven,
but sand-scoured, will still chatter its mandible.
We will feel the weight of all the earth, even as the sordid
slouch toward
Bethlehem. It is good you are dead, so they cannot see the
priggish staring
of your withered, disapproving eyes.

You long to trudge with them, though I, not being
desirous of such a pilgrimage,
settle comfortably next to your cadaver in the dark,
comparing parts.
My femurs are longer than yours,
but I envy how your phalanges are arrayed.

Our bones are both beautiful; though that one, well, his
hot eyes
devoured our fleshy fronts as if they were the same.

Sleepers in the Daylight

Grimace as I carry my French toast over to the table,
orange juice in one hand
—the natural sugars make my teeth ache.
The throb and acid nausea
signify routine's rubber band stretched too far,
as I look over Los Angeles International
spreading itself below my window
caught unawares in the unforgiving
sunlight of 7:30, 8:00 am.

We are normally dead at this hour.
We only see it when we stay up all night.

Its look is very 70s, I think,
the colors bright, but a hint of haze
bleached out. Overexposed.
We live as next-door neighbors to
500 some-odd flights to parts unknown per day
(but you seem proud to say you hold no passport).
The cockpits, silvered, gleam
in the damned eternal (tired?) sunlight,
but I watch the birds in our threadbare trees
and imagine a world much younger.

It hasn't been too long, in relative time,
that the planes have wrought havoc here.
They hang about, ripping apart the air,
feeding from the terminal's tubes,
gulping up transients for their fare.

A sip of orange juice. Lots of pulp,
the way we both like it.
But I have rubbed away the armor on my teeth,
sanded down the enamel,
scoured the exposed nerve,
and the sugar makes my teeth hurt.

What is Worth?

You say, "It isn't worth it."
but what is worth?
Is it simple value—like the twenty my fingers found
when they slid in my pants pocket?

I could take you out with that twenty,
if the time and drive were worth it to you.
Is it the afternoon spent scouring that mountain highway,
searching for the spot you found where we might watch a
sunset
when it got warmer, someday. Maybe?

You told me you "would take me home, if I had better things
to do"
than drive
in the shadow of the pines
with the windows down
for the first time that year
on quiet curving roads.
Is its currency the hours spent,
the light touches and simple gestures?

The small bright carton of blackberries you brought me one
morning
—that I ruined in the blender, anxious to extract
the best of all things from them, from you.

Was it the fading adrenaline in my veins,
when you grabbed my frozen hands
and led me along that snowy ledge?
Is it knowing that when this smooth calm is disrupted
like the surface of that lake by your skipping rocks
We could vanish?
Us, like the reflection of the trees and sky in the water.

These things, like forgotten bills in my back pocket until I
brush them with unknowing fingertips, all frantic, beg the
question.

Begone, Girl

The smell of exhaust exists
everywhere, uptown and down
and the scent of the Purina factory
miles off, permeates
a city increasingly cobblestoned.
Neighborhoods swelling and splitting
an almost bacterial procreation
but much like the gut
"beneficial flora!"
new and newer
and regurgitated.

No city can be organic, truly
but like many things it is fun
to watch it grow without
interference or assistance from me.
I am on safari
growing steel haired (in my mind)
my assortment of linen trousers
won't keep me warm in winter.
(Is it Spring yet?)

Observe or partake?

I want to be a part, apart.
I like it here, now that I don't need you.

Visiting and revisiting,
I'm weaving these threads into a rope
with which to hang myself.
We had good times.
The scent memories: rain, and dal chawal.
It was fall and the trees in the Highlands
were a riot of color
my thoughts turn to the last time
the weather romped untamed
and the rain caught us unawares.

Driving to the top of Lookout Mountain's overlook
and us two crashing waves
boiling, brash
trying to merge in your car's front seat
every moment we spent together
I felt an electric live wire coursing in my nerves
so dire—thrilled you wanted me
(the intensity was a red flag, I think)
or maybe I had grown fearful of good feeling
much the same way I've grown desensitized

to the way strange men approach me at the bus stop
alcohol reek aversion
that the later offer of wine and beer would offput

I'm unsettled daily, pressing my ambitions into pace
with the urban expansion
cross and discomfited at the ample distraction
of handsome men out of my reach
(and some within it
—perception or delusion?)
I want to go sink into the leaves at the lake
lie there, let some enterprising children cover me up
bury me alive in gold brown.
It's called Colorado
it once meant "colored" like skin, not "colored red,"
Imperialist history from the local newscaster.
I'm not even fluent but I can feel
the missing Maya beat
the geographic displacement
a culture shifted and inured
I miss home, but California is aflame
and my mother's packed up my personal torches
all that's left are the books gathering my brother's dust.

How have I gone so long
without being long gone
from here?

The Dying Year

It's fresh—the memory, the wound.
Red fresh, liquid—the dying year.

The distinction is arbitrary, calendar lines
    George, Julian, Maya
    bleed, bleed, bleed
but it is tangible, collect.
It began, and perhaps shall end
    —the dying year.

It declined in January: jaundiced sunlight,
coughed through June.
    You only got sick twice, you know,
    though you stayed in bed all day.
It was characterized by The Head Ache,
melancholia as usual; but a deeper sense
of fading away sunk in.

Right between the lungs and trachea,
between gills and gullet.
Panic—the cold stone—crept in.

Your hands shake even now, even
now. It is not December anymore.
Is it still the dying year?
You did not tell them of the
faint throb of varicose in
young cellulitic thigh, the memory
of skin supple enough to stretch and snap back.
    The two weeks when you couldn't
    stand to eat, in the dying year.

Failing and almost failing
Collegia, [in the dying year]
an incompletely drawn stagnant pond.
Sympathy Cs, passing grades
suckered from a sweet woman
who cannot know your true fester,
    fester, in the dying year.

You methodically dissected your
right heel, studying the way
your skin striated.
Squamous cells peeeeeled right off,
like the chicken you no longer cook,

but you did not eat your shame,
  limping in the dying year.

You just cried, helpless on the LA streets,
cowed by high rise condos
unhoused raconteurs,
and brutes who tried to steal your kisses,
and would have succeeded
if self loathing and a bottle of cheap tequila
had preservative properties.

You ran from the dark engine
of despair, but did not win.

Run over, in the dying year.

Sparrow in the dark

The ice still thick on the pavers in the pre-dawn glow
luminescent raindrops tip the branches in the late month
the tree lights the city left up.

Second sided face of Janus' coin
is chill wind blowing through my tights.

My soul the little bird pecking delicately at the train stop
under a fluorescent light, softened by the coming sun.

Broken pipe/May 24/Death toll 97,672

Sliced fingers hover over dirty carpets,
desperate to scrape together commonality.
What has been shattered here is a vehicle
to lucent yellow edged haze,
a viscous and formative yolk
suspending the jittery dust feathered wings
of my anxiety bashing itself against this wall
erected in fear between ourselves and the outsider.

Unseeable and deadly after a liquor balm
cold comfort and hot night terrors,
I inhale and contain as I hope we all contain
not multitudes but probability,
after which Humpty Dumpty fell,
a vessel of uncertain and infinite possibility,
yellow ichor dripped all into the gutter
and dried as it will in the sun,
tacky, corroding the paint.

Crowning virulent glory juxtaposed
against the haloes of plastic tubing and machine
anointed in hydroxychloroquine, in paper vestments,
discarded saints, March feet first into cold storage,

no shuffling shall cross contaminate this mortal coil,
the shuttling of legion corpses' names darken broadsheets
grown lengthy and sparse with doublespeak.

Uncovered faces corpulent gaping and a spittle mist
in fine droplets beats the time of year long thin,
a hammered aegis of crushed hope,
moth wing wafer against the creeping plutonic stab,
it all drips and drains dry into cisterns overflowing,
which still grow deep as the pathetic void
of the oligarchal heart.

The Eye

Miraculous engineering of flesh aside
the eye is an unmoored spinning orb
of relativity and truth
captivate
misdirect
manipulate the softer
unarmored hearts

exposed, a vulnerability
to the unseen intrusive
naked, it cannot perceive
protected it is also blind

blue silicone suction of swim goggles
a saving grace
while fogged and obstructive

keep out
a virus
rubber bullets
tear gas

But to see!

To know by seeing
to trust the point of view
visions of calm, health, peace
injustice

yet burn from mourning
overwhelming openness of a world cloistered
my eye wreathed in a fiery corona
all seeing as the slitted Maiar
witness bodies falling
and I, willing to risk its loss
to see justice done.

Coexist

your loss does not need to war with my loss
as your pain does not need to war with my pain
but instead can enmesh and rub gently along together
the uncertainty of fingers of two hands entwined.
we can bind together these sheafs of existence
into a library of shared living
and together into the forward hurtle
and bumpy turbulence of days and weeks and years
just...be.

Crying to Phoebe Bridgers

"Funeral" came on, and, unconsciously,
I released the internal pressure valve
of grieving for the hardness of the world.

The day started empty white,
filled up red with bleeding—a liquid crawl up a paper napkin
when I cleaned Tuscan white bean salad off the street.

It was lost on the pavement.
My flailing limbs sent it flying as my ankle disassembled
and shattered my pointe shoe hopes,

which I consoled with consumption.
The justice of a world without gods, without fate,
is cruel, inconsistent, maybe absent.

My troubles are laughable, insincere.
I see a man every day, chair bound, skull caved in,
still capable of speech and indignance,

at whom my traitor nerves and stomach do an atavistic turn,
and I look away.

Alone,
I let a begrudging tear fall for each recent death,
each systemic injustice, each small crack in my heart.

I pretended, as it happened
that I wasn't enjoying the chance to indulge myself
in the bone deep sadness I port around.

The pride is so heavy
and hard to carry, but if I put the ballast down
I might slip away, ungainly, in a breeze.

And too often ask
for help, for affection, comfort, solace, company.
To hear no, no, no, no, no.

Rejection a big fear,
bound up from small and petty woes
into an incense stick miasma.

I want to excise my heart
and throw the useless hunk of meat in the trash,
but refrain for people who are, even now, dying.
It might be needed.

Yellow irises

    —For Brianna Noble

Blades of grass on the first of June
the most vivid greens
poured into my eyes

grateful and dry they drank it up
four days of uncharacteristic tears
and crowd control agents

chartreuse soothing
verdant renewal shooting forth
from deeper shades

and irises in full bloom
a yellow so pale it's almost white
contrast to the common purple

beautiful as the neighbor's three blooms
the next day snipped
heads left in our front planters

the lighter irises grow sunny
less prey to the tyranny of greedy fingers
pinching away their lives.

One year, one half

There is no progress to report on my end
I haunt the empty houses of the better off
I drink their ethically sourced coffee on well-appointed patios
I sob into their well-groomed dogs
I read Adrienne Rich spread out in the sun
bronzing over the war between privilege and fear
for women who will never be free
the real decision never made

I shiver lonely in the rain and watch for cars and buses
still twisting and wringing out my love for you onto a yoga mat
but you are where my gaze naturally falls
the point to which my chest, my eyes, my hopes, my emotions
are oriented
Northwest now, the frigid Pacific of my youth touching your
Atlantic toes
which will not warm without me
I hope you haven't slept in 18 months
I am crushed beyond the time limit
desperate enough for a pharmaceutical solution

shattered by time's inconsequential passage
45 years later Adrienne's words are still true

and I could vomit my grief for this world endlessly
until more blood waters the earth for no real reason
Will we find each other? Have we found each other and yet are
still alone?
Still subject to the terrorists of the mind?
Still fraught with rage and hunger and helplessness
holding to a drishti of self-destruction the direction of the past

Romantic Notions

Funny, that it is considered romantic to declare
that you would die for love.
Living for love is much harder to do.

Ja Ara E

I am a trembling pillar
a confection waiting to collapse
any steadiness I display was
hard won
clawed with my fragile human nails
I dream often of growing talons

my unknowing oozed sexuality
a faulty light bulb flickering
the smirk I've always carried
more smug in my youth
now full and knowing and unsure
as the mysteries have deepened in me

but my moth eaten spirit drapes
not lifted by any wind
from each hole the slow unravel begun.

The Rats of Notre Dame

Squeaks and scampers
accompany the night music of the cathedral
exhausted from the weekend trample
of thousands of tourist feet

Gray bodies skitter
sleek through the night
and I try not to sigh again and contain
in my chest the outburst forming
like a storm cloud accumulates

He tells me in words accented that allure me
that there are few stray cats in Paris
but points out Jupiter (or maybe Saturn)
and shows me how to tell by the steadiness of light
if we are looking at a star or planet

I always assume they are airplanes, I say
and sip from my bottle of water, not wine
and wish we had spent each night of the past week
wandering together along the Seine

the water a glossy satin ribbon in the dark
beckons me to descend the stone steps
in the quai and surrender my body to
the embrace of an ancient city

the ache of three hours walking on cobbles
didn't diminish my desire to stay
the petulant sadness of soon-coming departure
dug claws into my chest and pricked my eyes

I looked so hard at the Haussmann architecture
gilded softly in the mellow amber of streetlights
I thought I might crack the stone
and with each inhale I hoped my lungs would retain
the mass of non-oxygen molecules and become heavy,
immovable

He would probably point out that such a thing would be fatal
and I would agree, inclined to be maudlin and absurd
this final midnight in my own placid, unintelligible heaven

Paris loved me back, maybe he would not have
and maybe it is best that I wasn't impulsive and foolish
and didn't try to stay

but my pulse warmed my veins
as he kissed me solemnly on each cheek
and then was gone

Stages

I.   Denial

I supplement the lack of you
with sips and starts
a conversant trickle
firing off quick messages
sent with fear and hope
of the response

I battled on the bloody plain
of others' opinions
for your honor

because you never hurt me
on purpose
indifference not malicious

Give me answers
how could you
spend the time
touch me so
stare into my eyes
caress my face

reject my soul

inexplicable

II.   Anger

I want to wind my vengeful fingers
around your beautiful neck
bite your cheek and tear off the flesh
consume you, feel you within me
the only way I can

how *dare* you
say you love me

III.   Bargaining

I will be good, so pure
I will crawl through a desert
change my fate
diet
bear your children

I can't become someone else

but I can change in your eyes
see me

see me

I am vast and unknowable to you
find me in my own depths
fathoms compress it all
into easily conveyed facts
flat
on paper, we are perfect
I can't acquire the skill
origami
and a sharp exhale to inflate
release into the sky

IV.   Depression

V.   ~~Acceptance~~

Waxing Crescent — Winter

It's cold enough to freeze tonight
but the concrete ribbon I walk is solid
like I balance along the bones of the earth

bordered by untouched snow
which throws off glints and glimmers
sugar under the street lamps

I trust that the cold concrete will be solid
grip the bottom of my ugly boots
I walk tall and fearless and alone

past a couple in the dark
who hold each other tight to keep warm
while I trudge through years of you
freezing temperatures, financial disappointment

the moon's chip sliver is usually my lodestone
but tonight a sly Cheshire grin hangs over me
better to be an axe head at this rate
I'll shatter before the freeze lifts
crystallized in fractal patterns
shadow stretched across the cold pavement

Void

There is a roundness to the sound
of the Tibetan singing bowl
a harmonic ring, assonant
reminiscent of the o in the ohm

the positive and negative of nothing
peace as you deflate each lung
panic as you run out of air

as the frigid dark resounds when you walk alone
as the night-sound calm descends

the whiteness and want of release
the darkness and fear of the pit

opposite sides of an absent coin
weighing heavy in a pocket

and as a historical concept, pangaeic
all came to know nothing.

What makes you leave

I lent him "Milk and Honey"
before I had read it myself.
Brand new, the sticker still on it,
because he was so beautiful it hurt,
and his asking had lit a fire.

He read it and then he left me.
Maybe there was a realization he found
—like how I ache now, the first read through.

The next one who asked to borrow I refused.
I didn't plan to keep him,
but if poetry will make him leave
it had better be mine.

Coffee and strawberries

coffee and strawberries
in the hot lateness of afternoon
make strange bedfellows in my gut
acid and bile rise
what humors
black and yellow
melancholia to erode
choleric to inflame
my anger and sadness
at this latest disappointment
a millstone at my neck
toss me in the mossy pond
my craft would make me float
but I've declined to continue
opting for this wooden half life
staring into middle distance
cold ceramic mug to lips, bitter then sweet
the bright red skin split
in due time, past time
I hope the thousands of tiny black seeds
take root in the miles of twists and turns
an undiscovered utopia
already colonized and staked

each time I let them in my body
a water wheel turning each time
I rise and fall each revolution
my spirits break over it
and I return again to the bottom
but it is early summer
and bereft of you
the berry yield is high and bright
and the coffee never runs out

Immutable Feast

Scorched earth
my two signs circle
bull and lion grapple
hoof and claw
yet both fixed
no roiling internal conflict
to shift my spirit into mutability

I caveat and dissemble
qualify and do not
my interest in the stars
an embarrassment to myself
but for the beauty
of the astrolabe in your eyes

regal and grounded
is the expectation
and the false perception
yet I am a hollow
a hungry ghost
consuming all and writing little

I make a meal of it
or two, or three
obsession a scald
burning my belly, mouth, hands
grasping against the scarcity
swallowing air

Slime

I cracked, and the albumen drip
left tiny patters in the void

Everything soft focused
48 hours behind tissue paper
dissociation a cushion from
pain, fear, exhaustion
can I survive another year?

My bold admission of darkness
danger, a warning I had dropped
a deep hole unfilled
saltwater, a frequent buoy
but quickly evaporative
vanished, the salt rime
a ghost, like I
to psychiatry
employment

The flattening of my countenance broken
the sun burst through the clouds
garish, refracted from snowclad trees
sickening brightness

Reds and yellows and whites
blood and yolk and serum
the slime, she called it, in our brains
fed the colors of the neon sign
my capitalist Christian Mecca of dead meat
undercooked potatoes, onions and spread

Pierce my heart with an oversized safety pin
and let the apron fall into the dirt
sow the food into the earth
and let the rabid dogs each succumb
to the poisoning
and no one to front eleven hundred dollars in tests
force the antibiotics down a toothy maw
bear the stench of wet dog food
usually an omen of an oncoming storm

Its aftermath a gloomy balm on the spirit
trees a frosted confection from my window
my soul in the mourning
inflammation soothed under a blanket of snow
and the scent of the blanket over the radiator
and the taste of chicory
and the airing of my grievances, my loss

Sterile

Skin has many layers
deciduous with the application of the right solvent

judiciously applied
remove peel scrub slough

scrutiny searing
did you wear a mask
how many were there

billions, subocular
almost incomprehensible
how we eat drink and breathe
without paralysis

my mother's chlorinated lungs damned
damaged goods you can't discard

How care you now?
Phillip Morris vindicated by a smoker's resistance
but paid our bills for how long

pubescent commercial labor
youth smoking prevention
and national sports

the exploitation of my youth
and the isolation of my age

No Left; Child Behind.

These days, lost in conversations,
I feel we eat the pie by spooning off the crust.
I aim my deprived orphan stare at
abandoned, filling-smeared plates.

In my mind's eye it's berry red—a tall poppy,
Illicit,
gutted, bloody articulation.

O Academia! (Oh, macadamia?)
No wonder Faustus scorned you. (Who?)
The buxom hetaera (hetero-what?)
promised to yield the bare.
(I think you've got something there!)

Dead-eyed genius, where hide you your
fat tongue? Salted, it cringes—a mollusk shrivel.

These days, lost in conversions,
I cannot decide if I want the pie
and the mug of the one percent
or 99 problems and willful deprivation.

—But God, how I hate waste.

Fatigue

Bless the sight of lightning from above
and a moon hung sickle
—a wall ornament off center.

From that bug eyed vantage
the fuselage a carapace
the horizon shrunk and laid bare

bypass the night, chase the sunrise
an orange streak above the smoky cloud layer
of morning thunderstorms.

I nod and startle,
fighting sleep as though it is that final rest.

Blood streams

They scream behind me: livid, joyous.
Shaking signs, weapons, banners.
I do not know
the woman shamed, the woman kept.
Spittle flecks spew from flapping maws.
They will burden me, bury me
devour my sandwiches.

I haven't baked any bread in weeks

they howl with acrimonious laughter
gaping mouths with obelisk teeth

my savage monthly redness paints their cheeks

but I bleed for civilization.
I bleed an intellectual.
I am, in all manners,
a manufacturer of all but lies.

Flight Attending

I.

You gotta get right with God, my mother says
that sometimes God is a cup of coffee.
Maybe she means the peace folks find under steeples.
Deity doesn't mean much to me at 38,000 feet.

Sometimes it's a pasta construct
when everything is absurd,
or it's a disapproving father
all strong hands and voice and plaid shirt
with the sleeves rolled up.

Maybe a god sent me these kittens,
mewing helplessly on this flight.
They have no concept of me,
I am uncleaved and unobserved
—heathen servant to the metal birds.

II.

The desperation of being alone
after only one week

draws my stare to men's sternums,
seeking the hollow place in their arms,
longing to be allowed in.

Homeless, I hop across the map
dotted lines ellipsing,
city to city.
The plane engine roar
and surge and that tingling feeling
each time we take to the sky
—blue, vast, endless,
devoid of deity.

Hunger

Hunger gets me out of bed
drives me
saps me of will.

My appetite diminished is a harbinger
of sad orange light times
—eye strain in the dawn.

But a bright day on snowy sidewalks
and the orderly modern renovations
on my building, prisonlike with a green accent
the doors, anxious to be opened.

Music is a pleasing melody
stomach acid rumbles
drives me with a sense of renewal
—optimism before noon.

I want to bite into the flesh of life
gently, humane.
Hunger makes me modern
and man, can I eat.

The appetite eludes me sometimes
but not today
as the days grow longer
and the snow is promised
to melt.

I am in love with sad jazz and myself
and the swift amnesia of dark humours
and the hungers that I have.

Restraint

My soul craves freedom
subzero blue skies
the flat carpeted platform roar
shaking my cells minutely
aloft only by the rending of the air

but also shrinking
cowardly in open spaces
throat a psychosomatic ache
histamine or viral intruder
impossible to know, like faces via screen

how is your heart faring
each beat stressed
sickness dying death
by covid or cop
enlarged, encapsulating

the names of the dead
are a pharmaceutical receipt
unfurling like the orange lilies
and the stately foxgloves
my eyes water for both.

Skyline view

Aching chips away at me still
day by day
and the light slips behind the mountains
and the storm clouds coalesce
and I can't sleep like I used to

the sunset burns the horizon
purple and gray, a bruised and dying muscle
electric like the tingles of withdrawal I feel
it's not working anyway
the pills aren't working anymore

I work three jobs for starvation wages
and I just want you, only you
a supplement to my malnourished brain
that threatens migraines daily
and I redirect my attention

out the windows at my back
twenty stories into thin air
rarefied sights for wealthy marks
I have no heart

no sense of privilege anymore
interloper that I am, you understood

how do I have room to miss you
in this brain stuffed full of cotton
I'm a fraction of myself
putting out multiples in product
draining myself dry

one day I'll fall and bust open
and sand will spill out of my skull
and as sand does it'll get into everything
and you'll find bits of it forever.

La Vitesse

Elation pedaled me home on your borrowed bike
the speed with which I am becoming besotted
my wits a soggy paper bag and yours a jet spray

I am all heart eyes and empty wallet

The velocity of my heart pounding in your direction
pulverizes the rib bones into fine sand
and stretches the skin of my chest

The pain of which is at turns pleasant and paralyzing
my mind races my rationale
on the curved embankments of my veins

My fingers shake, pulse uncontrolled
this fire hydrant ventricular act
propels me down the twilit street

Doomscrolling

I turn on an album
the file worn thin with listening
and thick where I have embroidered
myself into the liner notes
or whatever replaced them
I try to read—bell hooks
and though I am *all about love*
I pivot to flipping as if possessed
app to unseen app
I watch a man pour hot oil over a fish skin
and I watch him sew up the fish skin
and I know the image
fried scales flexing a hundredfold
will stay with me a while

Promise me winter is waning

Promise me spring
as snow is kissing the trees
I crave the vicious thrust
of green spikes sheltering
warmth. Oh, please, please

break the earth with verdancy
blow up the trunks and branches
boiling sap caused to sag
bake my skin to blister
set fire to my sinuses

beat away the winter birds
scream a summoning
for bloody foaling
shatter the shells
slick down sunny in slime.

In my dreams I am a runner

In my dreams I am a runner
I course along imaginary roads
the same few cities each night
a consistent oneiro-geography.

On the day before Christmas
I learned the h in harina is silent
how my anguish does not speak.

I have become the two quarters rattling
underneath the tamale pot steamer basket
I can only stop when there is no water left.

In my nightmares I heave dried corn meal
I look for you under rocks and floorboards
awake, I wonder if I need anyone.

Two broken ankles from a fall
an oath to never climb the walls again
but your silence foments arachnid madness.

In my dream I walked toward you
brand new on old feet, ravenous

buried my hands in your hair
and turned myself inside out.

Lilacs in the alley

It's green and bathwater warm,
the alley weeds are blooming,
I've moved into a bigger place,
and I might love again.

My heart, like my habitat,
has grown, and I consider;
there is room and reason for
opening myself up.

Pale violet flowers in the alley
and the high and head rush
from seeing you anew.

Uncaring that the fall,
come hard and cold,
will kill our love and lilacs both.

I've learned to speak to grieving

Hollow and heavy stone
lump and burning
throat and eyes
both closed and wrenched open

a thousand ways woven
to say
I am sorry you have lost

my knowledge of grief came late
and forcibly I held it
in my resistant mind
and found no comfort

I enter the dark room of memory
to behold the lights far off
drowning sadness for love lost
press down against it

use words to craft a hook
to fish you from the deeps
place you in shallow waters

still sodden
but closer to those lights.

When we are all drowning

When we are all drowning
these tasks will cease to matter
submerged
dissolved into acidic slurry
and I will miss sliding my fingers
along your hair and the clean sky.

When we are all asphyxiated
I will no longer care to look in mirrors
your empty pockets immaterial
I'll have plucked the final leaf
from the last wilting plant
as it returns to the earth.

She is calling us
ringing a dinner bell, a klaxon
inaudible
if they have their way
our bodies will never stop moving
never to alight gently
one last petal, to rest.

Field Log: Denver, 10 May

By the tenth of May the Denver trees
have begun to bloom and leaf
and it is green. So green I laugh, elated.
Some things I have seen:
flowers of six shades,
an alien—poppy in bloom, translucent
hairs cover the stalk and pod,
its neighboring flower a violent red,
a swarm of black flies,
bearded irises proud spikes thrust into the air,
a beetle on its back.
Someone (I dislike) has written "fuck earth"
on the pavement and had it been me
it would have said "*fuck*, Earth"
reverently, the way lovers do.

If it comes

If it comes, let it come
let it float, nebulous into safe space
make a mooring
or don't
let it
is all I'm saying.

Control is an illusion
weighted blanket
suffocation
imagination stuck on two scenes
let it grow, change, die.

Let it die
release it to death
as you will, one day, release yourself
as you have with others
fingers forced open
all that is dropped to the floor
forgotten.

Let it fall if it must fall
and believe me that it must

it must fall
it is the rule of empires that
endings are beginnings
destruction can be beautiful
beauty can break you
your oft broken heart
set free with the knowledge
that beauty holds so little value
in the true course of things.

Acknowledgements & Thanks

Some of these poems have been previously published.
My gratitude extends eternally to the editors.

Across the Margin:
      "If it comes"
      "Field Log: Denver, 10 May"
      "When we are all drowning"

You Might Need To Hear This
      "Coexist"

Rigorous Magazine
      "The Eye"
      "The Rats of Notre Dame"

Praised by December anthology, Wingless Dreamer, 2021
      "Slime"

Sublunary Review:
      "Sparrow in the dark"
      "Flight Attending"

MORIA Literary Magazine:

    "What makes you leave"

petrichor magazine:

    "Broken pipe/May 24/Death toll 97,672"

    "Portrait of Anxiety (The Worm)"

    "Waxing Crescent - Winter"

Angel City Review:

    "No Left; Child Behind"

Mincing Words

    "Epitome"

    "Playa del Rey"

    "Crying to Phoebe Bridgers"

    "Ja Ara E"

    "Coffee and Strawberries"

    "Black Square Summer"

birdy. Magazine:

    "Stargazing at the Lake"

Victor Valley College Writing Contest:

    "What is Worth?"

    "I Sought Refuge Where The Rocks Cleft"

Thank you, thank you endlessly: Emily Perkovich, who brought this book to life, and everyone at Querencia. Tommy Blake, for press matchmaking, and edits. Thank you to nat raum, for being both my friend and the most useful person to know. To Eszter Takacs, for stoop time on Williams Street and four hours in the In-N-Out line and always being a source of awe and inspiration. Veronica Bennet, the best last minute tablemate I could have asked for. Rosie Accola, for all you do for others. Monica Prince, Rita Mookerjee, Jose Hernandez Diaz, SG Huerta, and Todd Dillard, for your kindness and hype.

Thank you to Seth Copeland of *petrichor*, N'Jyia Shelton of *Mincing Words*, to my educators, Stan Brown, Bryce Campbell, Tim Adell, and Gail Wronsky. Thank you to my dear Rainbow Ink Writers Guild – Arkay Ussery, Linda Hardie, Susan Palwick, Locke Wilder. Sorry about all of the second person present in here.

Thank you to my community – Sam Traggardh, for being my person, MJ Stacey, for always writing with me and baking for me, Marissa Kazemi, for matching my freak, Megan Derman, without whom I would not be here today, Josh Pfeil, for the consideration, and the roasting, Cesar Prieto, for whom I would get out of bed to jump a battery any time, Ro Murdock, for your fire, Rachel Lynn, for always saying what I'm thinking, Rachel Ledbetter, for planting so many seeds, Tyler Harmon, just on the other side of the wall, even now, Cara McHale, for biscuits and laughter and being so damn cool, Annie Marshall, you dynamo, and Melissa McCormick, for being endlessly compassionate.

Thank you to Jennifer Schmohe, for being my muse since we were 13. To Kelly Golden, my best cheerleader. To Ellen Golden, forever supportive and who would have loved to hold this book in her hands. To Tory Adkisson, who I look up to, and who edited a few early versions of these poems.

Thank you to all of my friends & family who read my little poems on the internet.

Erika Gill (they/them) lives, writes and builds community on unceded Tséstho'e (Cheyenne), Očhéthi Šakówiŋ, hinono'eino' biito'owu' (Arapaho), and Núu-agha-tʉvʉ-pʉ̱ (Ute) land in Denver, Colorado. Erika is the Editor in Chief of Alternative Milk Magazine, an independent biannual literary and art magazine. In different lives, Erika has been a flight attendant, social media manager, actor, bartender and a music journalist. They grew up longest in Victorville, CA, which is notable only in being the filming location of *The Hills Have Eyes*. Erika's poetry may be found in *Rigorous, MORIA, Birdy,* and other spaces. This is their first collection of poetry.

www.ingramcontent.com/pod-product-compliance
Lightning Source LLC
Chambersburg PA
CBHW071533120626
46550CB00006B/2437

* 9 7 8 1 9 6 3 9 4 3 3 9 9 *